Original title:
Through the Island Mist

Copyright © 2025 Creative Arts Management OÜ
All rights reserved.

Author: Aurora Sinclair
ISBN HARDBACK: 978-1-80581-568-6
ISBN PAPERBACK: 978-1-80581-095-7
ISBN EBOOK: 978-1-80581-568-6

Awakening to the Embrace of Haze

Woke up today, couldn't see my toes,
The fog had rolled in, like a sleepy nose.
Stumbled to breakfast, tripped on the cat,
He looked unbothered, just sat there fat.

The coffee was brewing, but where's the cup?
I poured it on cereal—crunch, then sup!
A spoonful of milk splashed right on my cheek,
I laughed at my morning, the haze made me weak.

Outside I ventured, lost in the white,
Thought I'd find sunshine, but it played shy tonight.
Met a confused seagull, doing a twirl,
He quacked me a riddle, I gave it a whirl.

The fog made me giggle, a tickle of glee,
Each step was a mystery; was it sand or a tree?
With each little stumble, the world felt so grand,
In the embrace of the haze, it's a whimsical land.

Phantoms of Nature's Serenity

Monkeys dance in their fine attire,
As seagulls jest, trying to conspire.
Crabs wear hats, they think they're cool,
While fish gossip like they're in school.

A squirrel holds a tea party wide,
Complaining that the nuts just hide.
The trees they chuckle in the breeze,
While flowers giggle, teasing bees.

Beneath the Surface of Gentle Fogs

Frogs in tuxedos leap and croak,
Planning pranks, they're quite the joke.
Snakes in shades, they slither on,
Whispering secrets from dusk till dawn.

A turtle's hat is far too grand,
As he races, oh what a stand!
Fish flip-flop in a dazzling show,
While otters clap, putting on a flow.

The Mirage of the Nurtured Coast

Pelicans sport their funky ties,
Trading feasts for silly fries.
Lobsters twerk upon the sand,
While jellyfish play their band.

Crabs debate who's the kingpin,
While shrimp dance for a chance to win.
The sun laughs down, a playful beam,
Nature's party, the best of dreams.

Timeless Stories in Wisps of Blue

A whale spins tall tales of old,
While dolphins jump, so brave and bold.
Seagulls squawk with gossip flair,
Claiming they spotted a fancy fair.

Whispers swirl among the waves,
As crabs discuss their silly braves.
Starfish plot the next big joke,
While seashells laugh, oh what a poke!

The Enchantment of Solitary Shores

A crab in a tuxedo wanders the sand,
Snipping at jokes made by a lazy band.
Seagulls squawk gossip from their lofty height,
While a clam grins wide at the comical sight.

The waves break out laughing in foamy delight,
As fish toss around tales of their big catch fight.
A turtle in shades rolls his eyes and will say,
"Just another wacky, wavy day!"

Musings of a Shrouded Dawn

Misty shadows dance on the sleepy bay,
While a dolphin pretends he's a seal for the day.
The sun winks slowly, a bright golden tease,
As crabs scuttle past in their goofy, odd ease.

A rooster, confused, crows at the fog,
Startling a cow in an old wooden bog.
With a flick of its tail and a huff of a snort,
The cow mumbles back, "That's not my report!"

Serene Vistas Behind a Fogged Veil

The fog rolls in thick, like a blanket of dreams,
"Where are my keys?" shouts a sailor who beams.
His compass spins round in a dizzying whirr,
While a fish on a line says, "Hey, what's the blurr?"

A pirate emerges, half lost in the mist,
Searching for treasure he's sure he won't list.
With a wink and a laugh, he says with some glee,
"Where's the best place for a fine cup of tea?"

Mystic Shores of the Whispering Sea

A sandcastle tumbles, it sighs and it moans,
As children declare it their throne of dry bones.
The tide gently giggles, the shore shifts and shakes,
While a walrus declares, "For goodness' sakes!"

From the depths of the waves, a mermaid protests,
"Can you kindly keep quiet? I just need my rest!"
With a flip of her tail and a roll of her eyes,
She drifts back to sleep, to her watery skies.

Symphony of Softest Echoes

In a place where sea gulls chat,
A crab danced like a drunken brat.
Shells scattered, but they took a trip,
Rolling merrily, a lively skip.

Grasshoppers laughed on the swaying vines,
Singing tunes of sticky lines.
Fish wore hats and flipped with glee,
Who knew the ocean had a jamboree?

Fragments of Light in the Fog

A lighthouse sneezed in bright delight,
Waves giggled soft, in the fading light.
Seagulls strutted like they owned the shore,
Who knew clouds could create such a lore?

The lighthouse beam, oh what a jest,
Dancing around like a party guest.
Barnacles sported little top hats,
Cracked jokes with the curious cats.

The Canvas of Dewy Horizon

Morning dew painted with a wink,
Fish in slippers began to think.
Waves whispered secrets to the sand,
While turtles moonwalked, quite unplanned.

Clouds played hide and seek with the sun,
As spoons held dances, oh what fun!
A painter's brush? No, just a dog,
Chasing its tail in the swirling fog.

Shimmering Veils over Ancient Rocks

Rocks in robes of misty lace,
Giggled and swooned in a clumsy chase.
Tortoises rolled with a comical flair,
Sipping sea air without a care.

The waves clapped hands, a watery show,
As otters twirled in a daring flow.
A seaweed wig waved to the breeze,
While shells chuckled and squeaked with ease.

Wandering Spirits of the Salt-Sprayed Isle

A ghostly crab in flip-flops ran,
Chasing after a jolly tan.
He slipped and fell in a seaweed patch,
Declaring, "I'm the coolest—what a catch!"

The seagulls cawed their raucous cheer,
"Hey, Mr. Crab, it's not that dear!"
With a wink and a nod, he made a dash,
Saying, "Next time, I'll take a splash!"

Wistful Echoes in the Warm Embrace

A parrot perched on a coconut tree,
Whispered jokes to the bumblebee.
"Knock, knock! Who's there?" he squawked with glee,
The bee buzzed back, "Honey, is it me?"

Waves rolled in with a playful roar,
Telling tales of pirates and more.
But the crabs grumbled, "We've heard it all,
Can't we just go for a beach ball?"

Stories Latent in the Rolling Mist

In the thick of the haze, a turtle grinned,
Said, "I've got stories that never end.
Once I raced a hare, or so I claim,
Though he got bored and left the game!"

Beneath a jokester's moon so bright,
Squids wiggled about in sheer delight.
"Who's got the snacks?" they all did cheer,
As they danced amongst the jellyfish sphere.

The Breath of Secrets on Salted Winds

The winds whispered secrets in cheeky tones,
About a cat who danced on clam shells' thrones.
He wore a hat made of seaweed lace,
And dreamed of being the ocean's ace.

A walrus chuckled, "Come join my crew!
We'll wear silly hats and jump in too!"
But the cat meowed, "I think I'll pass,
I've got a date with a beachside glass!"

Reflections in the Shimmering Mist

A seagull stole my sandwich, oh dear,
With a laugh, it took off, feeling no fear.
I chased it down the beach, my face full of frowns,
But he just soared high, wearing culinary crowns.

The waves giggle softly, a comical crew,
They splash at my ankles, whispering, "Boo!"
I dance like a fool to their teasing tunes,
While crabs join the party, sporting shiny balloons.

Secrets of the Wandering Tide

The tide came in wearing mismatched socks,
I laughed so hard, my flip-flops lost their locks.
A starfish waved hello with a starry grin,
While a clam winked at me, as I tumbled in.

A dolphin in shades did a flip and a dive,
Said, "Life is a beach, let's feel truly alive!"
With each splash and each laugh, we danced in delight,
As the ocean whispered secrets deep into night.

A Diary of Whispering Winds

The wind has a secret, I know it's true,
It carries my hair in a wild, crazy stew.
It danced through the trees, tickling their leaves,
While I stumbled behind, yelling, "Can't you believe?"

A kite tried to escape, but got caught in a vine,
It wiggled and jiggled, saying, "Oh, I'm just fine!"
The sun set in beams of orange and gold,
And we laughed at the stories the night would hold.

Haunting Melodies of Salted Air

The fog sang a tune that I couldn't quite catch,
All I heard was a hiccup, a raspy old scratch.
The pelicans pranked me, dropping my hat,
While I stood looking silly, just what's up with that?

The salty breeze chuckled, lifting my spray,
It whispered sweet nonsense, then danced away.
As I sang with the gulls, off-key and absurd,
The waves rolled their eyes, saying I'm quite the nerd!

Sighs from the Mystic Depths

In the shrouded bay, a catfish grins,
Wearing a bowtie, he invites you in.
Mermaids giggle, they toss their hair,
With bubbles like popcorn that float in the air.

A crab with a monocle sips on his tea,
Claiming he's cultured, just wait and see!
But his caviar's really just jellybeans,
As he waves to the squid in his fancy sheens.

The octopus juggles with flair and finesse,
While fish in tuxedos create quite the mess.
They all dance around, a slippery ball,
Even the seaweed joins in with a call.

So join in the laughter, the fun never ends,
In depths where the water and whimsy blend.
With a wink and a splash, the show's not quite done,
Just wait till the plankton join in for the fun!

Enchanted Loam Awash with Fog

In a garden of dreams where the gnomes play chess,
They argue for hours, but it's all just a mess.
One claims he's the king, with a crown made of snails,
While the others just chuckle, trading tall tales.

The toadstools are lively, they dance in a row,
With glimmers of mischief, putting on a show.
A wind-up frog hops, with each boing and bounce,
Till he lands in a puddle—oh, what a flounce!

A pixie complains, 'My wings are too sticky!'
While a squirrel in boots thinks he's looking so tricky.
He twirls in circles, though he sees it as bold,
But his dance is a flop, and his nuts he has sold.

So wander the trails through the fog and the mirth,
Among enchanted critters, all full of worth.
In twilight's embrace, where whimsy feels right,
Every giggle and chuckle is pure delight!

Murky Glimmers of Forgotten Lore

Along the old path, the shadows do creep,
Where ghosts tell stories as the others sleep.
A pirate's lost sock causes quite the stir,
As the mermaids all chuckle, 'What an odd blur!'

A dog with a parrot claims he can fly,
With his aviator goggles, oh my, oh my!
He leaps off a rock, but just lands with a splash,
While the parrot squawks loudly, 'You made quite the crash!'

Moonbeams reveal secrets in puddles of goo,
Where frogs wear sunglasses, and some sip on stew.
They croak jokes with a flair, oh my, what a sight,
As faeries flap by, giggling into the night.

So gather your friends in this land of surprise,
Where legends are born, and laughter's the prize.
In murky yet charming spaces, be bold,
For magic's afoot, with treasures to hold!

Celestial Echoes Above the Water

Beneath the bright stars, the moon starts to grin,
While fish play charades, trying hard not to win.
A seagull takes bets on who will take flight,
As a dolphin leaps up with all of his might.

'Look, I'm a rocket!' a crab starts to claim,
As he wiggles and giggles in a loud funny game.
But he trips on a shell, falls flat on his face,
And the tide rolls in, giving him quite the race!

The stars whisper secrets to the waves below,
While starfish in hats put on quite a show.
They twirl and they spin, with glittering grace,
As the silly sea creatures all join in the chase.

So raise up a toast to the joy and surprise,
In the echoes of laughter, where silliness lies.
Under a blanket of starlit delight,
The ocean's a party, oh what a night!

The Wandering Heart Beneath Mist

A heart that skips, a silly beat,
In foggy shoes, it trips on feet.
With every leap, it laughs and sings,
To follow dreams, that silly thing.

It rolls and tumbles, much too free,
A love struck fool, as you can see.
Chasing shadows, missing lunch,
Mirthful giggles, oh what a bunch!

In playful dance, the heart's delight,
Through vapor trails, it takes to flight.
With puffed up cheeks and windswept hair,
It stumbles home, a breath of air.

Yet as it fades into the night,
The heart whispers secrets, pure and bright.
A wanderer lost, but not forlorn,
In every blush, a joy reborn.

Soft Footsteps on the Moistened Sand

With wiggly toes on sandy ground,
Soft footprints make a splashing sound.
Each step a giggle, a playful dash,
Like frolicking ducks, a silly splash!

The tide rolls in, a sneaky foe,
It chases me, oh what a show!
In salty puddles, I trip and flop,
A dance of joy, I cannot stop!

The sea calls out, a tickling tease,
As jellyfish wiggle with so much ease.
I leap and sway, a coastal prank,
With every splash, I giggle, crank!

So here I glide, on the silky shore,
Barefoot antics, forevermore.
In ocean's laugh, my spirit flies,
A jellybean heart beneath soft skies.

Ethereal Lights in the Enveloping Mist

In the fog, a flicker glows,
Like fireflies dancing in silly rows.
They twirl with glee, a charming sight,
Creating chuckles in the night.

A glow of giggles, a wink so bright,
As they play tag with the shroud of night.
Each sparkle whispers a flick of fate,
In a playful jig, they hesitate.

Suddenly hush, a wobbly beam,
It trips on shadows, a wobbly dream.
With a flick of laughter, it swoops and spins,
While the moon just chuckles and grins.

These lights of laughter play hide and seek,
Frolicking gently, mystique unique.
In the swirling haze, mischief unfurls,
As an ethereal dance wraps around the world.

Nocturnal Embrace of the Sea

The sea whispers secrets in moonlit waves,
While I try to listen from sandy caves.
With giddy delight, it dances around,
A cheeky frolic on the misty ground.

It tickles my toes, a playful tease,
As I splash back, feeling at ease.
With starry giggles, the night holds tight,
In watery arms, we laugh with delight.

The moon just beams with a silver grin,
As I splash about, losing my chin.
In a silly waltz, I'm caught by surprise,
With salty snickers that sparkle and rise.

So here's to the night, with the waves so free,
In a playful embrace between you and me.
With joy soaking in every merry line,
Let's twirl with the tide, in moments divine!

Mysteries Among the Driftwood

Lost socks mingle with seaweed,
A crab steals my sandwich, oh dear!
Seagulls squawk in a choir offbeat,
While I chase my hat in sheer fear.

An old boat whispers its secrets,
Its ghost sails high on a breeze,
It tips over like my breakfast,
Now I'm stealthy as clumsy bees.

Wooden faces carved with odd glee,
Lurking in shadows, they wave at me,
I laugh with a twig in my beard,
Who knew driftwood could be so weird?

A treasure map drawn in the sand,
Turns out it's just a cat's paw print,
Adventure awaits in this land,
But first, let's just find my lost tint.

The Horizon's Soft Embrace

The sun dips low, a pillow of gold,
Pigeons prance, acting all bold,
They chase crabs on a sandy dance,
While I try to catch my lost pants.

A beach ball sails through the air,
Hit by a wave, it's now a dare,
The horizon giggles and winks,
As I tumble in, covered in kinks.

Seashells whisper their silly stories,
Of fish who dream of land glories,
While sandcastles start to sag,
Shaped like a life with a bit of a lag.

A dolphin dives with a joyous twist,
It leaps out and gives me a kiss,
Magic's here, wrapped in a wave,
But seriously, where's that brave?

Dreams Cradled by Seafoam

A jellyfish with a polka dot hat,
Says, "Join our dance, it'll be a splat!"
We twirl and swirl beneath the sun,
With tangles of seaweed, oh what fun!

Mermaids giggle and splash about,
They throw sea shells with a playful shout,
I join their folk dance, trip on a clam,
And land in a puddle with all the jam.

Clouds are marshmallows drifting by,
As I snarfle down chips—oh my!
The waves chuckle, splashing my toes,
Telling me secrets only sea knows.

A starfish greets me with a wave,
Says, "Life's a joke; be silly and brave!"
With dreams adrift on bubbly foam,
I find my joy, my giggly home.

The Quiet Call of Distant Waves

The waves whisper tales of boats gone astray,
A rubber duck floats, claiming the bay,
It nods as if something's afoot,
Perhaps it's plotting, or just plain cute.

Sand gophers peek with curious eyes,
They hold tiny meetings, discussing the pies,
While I search for critters in my flip-flops,
Waves crash laughing as my foot drops.

A coconut rolls by, sporting shades,
It claims it's the king of the parades,
I bow to the nut, it winks in delight,
As seagulls make fun of my moonlight flight.

Tunes of the ocean, a silly refrain,
I join in the chorus, embracing the rain,
With bubbles around, life's a rib-tickling race,
Here on the shore, I find my place!

Echoing Whispers in the Fog

A seagull squawked, what a hoot,
He stole my sandwich, oh what a brute!
The fog rolled in like a thick, warm blanket,
And left our picnic all in a shank it.

We wandered lost with giggles and glee,
Tripped over roots, oh what a spree!
The lighthouse blinked, its light was a tease,
It must have known how to crack the breeze.

A crab did dance with a jellyfish prayer,
While fish played tag without a care.
We laughed so hard, the mist turned to cheer,
In the island's grip, we lost track of the year.

At dusk, we spotted a strange little frog,
He croaked a tune, how it made us blog!
A night full of wonder, with giggles in tow,
We'll come back again, but this time, less slow!

The Isle of Serene Secrets

Beneath the trees, where shadows play,
We claimed the beach without delay.
A hermit crab wore my lost sock,
As if it was style, oh what a shock!

In twilight's glow, the crickets sang,
Joined by the wind, what a silly clang.
The waves whispered tales, half-true, half-lie,
Of treasure chests and a parrot's eye.

The bamboo danced, a misfit crew,
While we skidded in puddles, like two wacky fools.
A treasure map led us far and wide,
Only to find a fake, and we almost cried!

With giggles echoing through the misty air,
We declared ourselves kings of the 'Silly Affair.'
A grand adventure painted in laughter's hue,
For secrets of the isle just mean more to pursue!

A Harmony of Misty Lullabies

A sleepy sheep counted the waves,
While dreaming of cabers and kitty braves.
In the haze, a dolphin gave chase,
And made quite the splash in our picnic space.

The moon peeked out with a blushing look,
As we played charades with a lost book.
A bottle drifted in, with a note inside,
It said, 'Find my sandals, they ran off to hide!'

With chortles and loud, we searched every nook,
Under the rocks and beside the brook.
A parakeet squawked, 'You're doing it wrong!'
As we sang our own tune, off-key, but strong.

The night fog thickened, a soft blanket cover,
Our laughter mingled, like a careless lover.
For in this harmony of silliness near,
Each misty lullaby brought jokes to cheer!

The Silent Call of the Waves

The waves whispered secrets, but oh so loud,
As we danced on the shore, feeling so proud.
With shells in our pockets and sand in our hair,
We played hide and seek without a care.

A starfish winked, said, 'Join my crew,'
But all he got were giggles and boo-hoos.
A rogue wave splashed, and our hats went flying,
The seagulls laughed while we stood crying.

The sun began to set, painting skies bright,
We chased after crabs, had a silly fight.
With every leap, our laughter rang true,
The silent call of waves drew us anew.

As nightfall gathered, we found a toad,
He croaked our favorite tune on the road.
We promised the island, with each crazy wave,
We'd keep coming back, it's the best place to misbehave!

Shrouded Paths of Silent Journeys

Coconuts roll down a lively hill,
Parrots gossip 'bout thrills and will.
Waves dance like they've lost a bet,
While crabs on the shore act overly wet.

Turtles wrestle in a slow-motion race,
As jellyfish float with a jelly-like grace.
Locals chuckle at the silly scene,
Where every creature has a whimsical sheen.

Distant boats tiptoe on the brew,
With captains who laugh and lakes that skew.
The sun teases clouds with a cheeky grin,
As mermaids wave, caressing the din.

So here we skip, in a merry mess,
Amongst the giggles, the sun's warm press.
Let the sea breeze whip our worries away,
In this carefree dance where the seafoam play.

Spirits of the Distant Isles

A parrot squawks a pirate's song,
While surfboards wobble all day long.
Ghostly figures laugh in the mist,
But they're really just locals with a sun-kissed twist.

Palm trees sway with a jazzy beat,
As iguanas strut with a stampede of feet.
They wear shades, feeling pretty cool,
While kids splash around in the shimmering pool.

Playful waves tickle the sandy shore,
As starfish smile, begging for more.
Dancing octopuses mime a swish,
In this fun zone, it's the ultimate wish.

So find your laugh in the salty air,
Where goofy spirits wander without a care.
With every sunset and fishy grin,
The magic continues, let the laughter spin.

Veiled Vistas of the Quiet Horizon

Under the blanket of a kaleidoscopic sky,
Sands whisper secrets as seagulls fly.
Wobbly umbrellas dodge the breeze,
As laughter bursts like coconuts from trees.

Old boats creak in a cheeky serenade,
Fish jump high, but they're too dismayed.
With whirlpools messing up a crab's good catch,
The ocean's antics are hard to match.

Sunsets spill colors that giggle and tease,
As fireflies glow with a squishy squeeze.
The horizon unfurls with a chuckle divine,
As the stars pop out to share some wine.

Here's to the breezes that tickle the soul,
In this joyous kingdom where all lose control.
Join the debauch of each wave and crest,
For in these mirthful moments, we are truly blessed.

Kinship with the Approaching Mist

Fog rolls in like a comedian's joke,
Hiding and seeking like a silly bloke.
Chasing shadows, the laughter ignites,
As beaches bubble with playful delights.

A dolphin twirls in a raucous spin,
Saying hello with a cheeky grin.
Local fishermen tell jokes at dawn,
While the mist wraps them like a fluffy yawn.

Shells spill tales of their salty bliss,
Each whispering secret is hard to miss.
With every giggle, a wave winks back,
In this lovely place where nothing lacks.

So let the fog tickle your toes and your nose,
Embrace the fun where the goofy wind blows.
In this comedy act of waves and tide,
Join the silly stroll, let the laughter abide.

The Solitude of Dappled Shores

On dappled shores we dance around,
With jellyfish wearing crowns, oh what a sound!
The crabs join in, with sideways strut,
While seagulls squawk as if in a rut.

Shells are secrets, whispered soft,
Each one hoping for a lift-off.
But we just laugh, at their shy retreat,
In sun-soaked chaos, we find our beat.

The tides bring tales of fishy winks,
With seaweed wigs that bring us kinks.
The sea foam giggles, we can't resist,
As we poke and prod this watery mist.

So here on the sands, we boldly play,
In goofy splashes, we spin in sway.
For solitude's just a funny disguise,
Under the sun, with laughter that flies.

Dreams Woven in Whispers of the Sea.

Underneath the moon's silver beam,
We float on dreams, or so it may seem.
A dolphin jokes, with a flip and a splash,
While crabs in tuxedos make quite the dash.

The waves share secrets of socked-up feet,
Where sea monsters serve us a rather neat treat.
Laughter echoes, as fish start to sing,
While mermaids giggle, their hair in a ring.

The sandcastles tower, but they start to squish,
As wave after wave makes a soggy wish.
Even the sand, with a chuckle or two,
Tries to tickle our toes, just to break through.

So let's cast our nets of humor and cheer,
With whispered wishes, and fun without fear.
For in this night's glow, we twirl and we sway,
In dreams woven tight, we dance 'til the day.

Veils of Coastal Whisper

Beneath veils of soft, breezy tease,
The seagulls plot, oh, such raucous degrees.
With waves as the backdrop, they dance and they dive,
While we giggle full-out, just feeling alive.

The tide rolls in with a sly, breezy grin,
Tickling our ankles, whispering in.
An octopus winks from his rocky demure,
As a flatfish grumbles, 'That'll never lure!'

In kelp's leafy embrace, we notice a show,
Of hermit crabs prancing—oh what a glow!
The shells are their costumes, all mismatched and wild,
In nature's grand carnival, oh how we smiled.

So here we sit, with our toes in the foam,
In a coastal comedy, we wiggle and roam.
For amidst all the whispers and secrets, we find,
The fun in the folly, with laughter entwined.

Secrets of the Sea Breeze

Sea breeze dances, with hints of delight,
As we chase waves, not caring for flight.
The fish all giggle at our clumsy grace,
While crabs play tag, all over the place.

Each wave comes crashing with a bubbly laugh,
As seashells declare their own autograph.
We poke and prod at the watery spritz,
Competing with seagulls, for fun little bits.

But then comes a splash, and oops, down we go,
In a swirl of foam, a slippery show.
With sand in our hair, we rise with a grin,
For the secrets exchanged, let the fun begin.

So let's hold the tales of the sea in our hearts,
With breezy giggles, and sunbeam arts.
For in this grand play of laughter and breeze,
The secrets we share are sure to please.

Ghosts of the Waters' Past

In the murky deep they play,
Old fish with tales of the bay.
They swam with glee, then took a dive,
Now they tell jokes, oh, to survive!

A crab with a top hat strikes a pose,
While seals line up to tickle their toes.
The jellyfish flash like disco balls,
And the clams cheer on in their pearly halls.

A mermaid's laugh echoes so bright,
As she dances with seaweed, what a sight!
Her fishy friends form quite the band,
With barnacles playing, all unplanned!

So if you dip your toes in the foam,
Expect a party, not just a roam.
For under the waves, hilarity's found,
Where laughter rises, crowned all around!

The Lullaby of Lost Horizons

From the cliffs, the fog whispers low,
Humming tunes where shipwrecks go.
A pirate's ghost jokes with a gull,
While dreams of treasure give a tugging pull.

The sun sets slowly, swinging wide,
As seagulls squawk, oh what a ride!
A vessel's anchor, it just won't quit,
Dancing around like it's having a fit.

With each wave crashing, the tales unwind,
A lighthouse keeper, a little maligned.
He fell asleep while the fog rolled in,
Woke up laughing at his own silly kin!

So sing along with the haunting breeze,
For on this coast, it's all about ease.
Where ghosts mingle and giggles last,
In the lively lull of the horizons past.

Secrets Held by the Rolling Fog

The mist arrives with a playful swoosh,
As coastlines giggle and waves whoosh.
A raccoon in a jacket, tipsy and spry,
Nibbles on snacks, as clouds drift by.

The seagulls gossip, tapping their feet,
While otters hold court, they can't be beat.
A turtle named Larry joins in the fun,
Winking at prawns as he basks in the sun.

The fog hides secrets, still they insist,
That laughter is truth; one can't resist.
They wave their fins, beckoning near,
Come join our band, let's share a cheer!

With patterns of light and shadowy ropes,
This thrilling hoot is what dreams hope.
In each bubble that pops from the tide,
Lurks a chuckle, a giggle, a humorous ride!

Ephemeral Glimpses of Nature's Breath

Nature's breath around us swirls,
As breezes weave and laughter twirls.
The branches shiver, tickled by cheer,
Even the rocks grin ear to ear.

A butterfly flutters, tripping on air,
Telling tall tales without a care.
While flowers shimmy with a giggly croon,
Dancing to rhythms of a sunny tune.

A wise old owl, perched up high,
Rolls his eyes at a snail rushing by.
"If you're in a hurry, you've missed the best,
Just slow down and enjoy this quest!"

So take a moment, breathe in delight,
As nature chuckles beneath the light.
For life's full of joys in every glance,
A chance to giggle, a chance to dance!

Mystic Silhouettes of Dawn

Shapes in fog arise, oh so sly,
They dance like shadows, oh my, oh my!
A seagull squawks, 'What's with the haze?'
While I trip on seaweed, in morning's maze.

Laughter echoes, as mist rolls away,
I chase a ghost crab, but it won't stay!
In the light, I see, it's a piece of toast,
Not a treasure chest – just my breakfast ghost!

The palm trees shrug, in the lazy morn,
Waving at me, like I'm 'twilight-born.'
With my silly hat, I strut and prance,
A vacation's spirit, in a goofy dance.

So here's to mornings, all fog and fun,
With mystic silhouettes, and laughter spun.
To forget the worries, take a whirl and sway,
In this silly paradise, it's a goofy day!

A Canvas of Mysterious Tones

Colors blend with a splash of glee,
A painter's palette, just for me!
I trip on paint, oh what a sight,
As I create a blue giraffe, so bright!

The waves brush whispers on the shore,
They giggle at footprints left before.
My brush slips and spills – oops! – what a mess,
Turning the dolphin into a dress!

Moods shift like the clouds in the sky,
My canvas grins as I pass by.
A parrot squawks, 'That's no good, mate!'
But I'm just here to celebrate!

So here's a toast to all that's strange,
Mysterious strokes, a funny range.
In this canvas world, so wild and bold,
I paint with laughter; it never gets old!

Beneath the Shroud of Dawn

Veils of mist play hide and seek,
Making me peek and then squeak!
Where's that crab, I thought he'd stay?
Oh wait, that's lunch—my sandwich, hey!

The sun tickles clouds with a golden hand,
As shadows mingle to form a band.
Drumming on seashells, a twilight show,
A laughter serenade, just go with the flow.

The coconut tree, it leans with glee,
Bending low to whisper to me.
'Watch your head!' it seems to sing,
But dodging fruit is a somersault thing!

So here's to the humor in dawn's embrace,
With giggles that follow, a whimsical trace.
No worries here, just light-hearted fun,
As I tumble through day—let the laughter run!

Ghostly Footprints in the Sand

Footprints appear, then vanish fast,
I follow a phantom, what a contrast!
"Sandy ghost, where do you roam?"
But it leads me back to my beachy home.

Beach towels flutter like ghosts in flight,
They wave at me, 'Come join the fright!'
A seagull cackles, thinking it's grand,
As I chase my hat across the sand.

The crabs have a party in a sandy hall,
With snacks of seaweed—oh, do not stall!
I'm ready to join, in this crazy dance,
Spilling my drink—oh, what a chance!

So here's to the laughter beneath the sun,
With ghostly antics, this day is fun.
Join the parade, with silly commands,
In a beachy world, with ghostly bands!

Whispers of the Celestial Ocean

In a boat made of foam, we floated and laughed,
Fish told us secrets, their fins were the craft.
Waves played a tune, a ridiculous jive,
We danced with the octopus, oh what a dive!

Seagulls were cackling, our snack they'd steal,
While crabs on the shore made a madcap appeal.
Shells whispered stories, soft as a breeze,
We chuckled at mermaids with algae for cheese.

The sun wore a hat made of jellybean rays,
As we slid on the sand in a spastic ballet.
Each tumble was laughter, each splat was delight,
We twirled like the seaweed, till fell the night.

In the water, we sang about fish in a trance,
The dolphins all joined, ready to dance.
With giggles and splashes, we waved goodbye,
To the silly shenanigans beneath the sky!

Tales Carved from the Misty Isle

Up on a cliff with a view oh so grand,
We spotted a crab who was boss of the sand.
He waved his one claw, as if to say,
"Join in my kingdom, come frolic and play!"

The fog rolled in thick, we could barely see,
A parrot named Pete, claimed he could speak for free.
With jokes that were silly, he'd flap and he'd squawk,
We laughed till we cried at his quirky old talk.

A pirate appeared, with a map upside down,
He sought for the treasure, but found just a frown.
We showed him the way, with a wink and a grin,
And led him to joy, now let the fun begin!

At sunset, we danced like the waves in the bay,
With stories of laughter, we banished the gray.
Tales carved from the mist, so wild and so bright,
A saga of silliness, wrapped in pure light.

The Silenced Song of Age-Old Roots

Trees whispered tales in a language of quirks,
With branches that jigged, the whole forest smirks.
Roots tangled and twisted, engaged in a jest,
While squirrels debated who made the best nest.

A turtle wore glasses, esteemed an old sage,
He lectured on wisdom from the prehistory page.
But with each word of advice, a cheeky little crow,
Would tease and would caw, saying, "Where's your hat, bro?"

Flowers were giggling, their petals aglow,
As beetles debated, who spun the best show.
In a whirl of confusion, the breeze took a turn,
And laughter erupted, a sweet twist of fern.

Under the moon, we all came to play,
With roots in a tangle, we laughed till the day.
The silenced songs melded, with humor so pure,
In the heart of the grove, we found our allure!

Hallowed Grounds of Misty Dreams

In a glade full of fog, we tripped on our toes,
With fairies that giggled, and noses like foes.
They tickled our sides with their tiny soft wings,
And sang us a tune of enchanted odd things.

A sloth in a top hat, so scholarly wise,
Explained to the moon how he packed to the skies.
We blinked in confusion, but laughed so we cried,
As he bored us to sleep while the fairies all pried.

Moss-covered rocks formed a podium grand,
For critters who battled all silly and planned.
With acorns for armor, they taunted and teased,
While laughter erupted, the evening appeased.

As night cloaked the ground, we reveled in schemes,
Where hallowed grounds shimmered with whimsical dreams.
In a whirlwind of joy, we twirled and we soared,
Creating our memories, never ignored!

Murmurs Beneath the Canopy

In the woods where the squirrels play,
I trip and stumble on my way,
Lost a shoe in a muddy prank,
Laughter echoes, my face is blank.

A raccoon steals my sandwich, oh dear!
It winks at me, then disappears,
Like shadows dancing without a care,
Where'd he go? I search everywhere.

Trees whisper gossip as I pass,
"Did you see her? She fell in the grass!"
But I just grin, it's all in fun,
Who knew getting lost would weigh a ton?

Yet the sun peeks through the green so mild,
As I chase the laughter, just a wild child,
With every tumble and every fall,
I make this place a carnival!

Island Dreams in a Soft Veil

Tiki torches dance, what a sight,
I set my drink down, oh what a fright!
A coconut rolls right off the stand,
And smacks a seagull, oh isn't life grand?

Beneath the palm trees, I kick up sand,
Pretending to have a rock band!
The crabs join in with their clawing beat,
While I'm the star, tapping my feet.

Mangoes fall like sweet confetti,
I dive to catch them — oh, so unsteady!
The beach is alive with giggles and cheers,
As I juggle fruit with no fears!

In this dreamy realm, I lose track of time,
Where everything's funny, and all's a rhyme,
With jokes in the breeze and laughter galore,
Oh, let's dance, who could ask for more?

Echoes of the Lost Shores

I walked the shoreline, searching for peace,
But tripped on a shell and made quite a scene,
The waves laughed out loud, rolling with glee,
As I washed my face in the briny sea.

Seagulls squawk secrets, I need to decode,
What's so funny? Their language explodes!
I try to join in, let out a squawk,
But all they do is mock and mock.

A treasure chest calls, I move to pursue,
And find it's just shoes, possibly two,
I wear them with style, call me "fancy toast,"
Nothing's more splendid than shoes that boast!

Lost shores present their silly allure,
With every slip, I feel quite secure,
For laughter's the melody that I will hum,
As I dance on the beach, oh what fun I've sprung!

Hidden Paths in Lush Green

Wandered paths covered in leaves,
Followed a frog while it weaves,
It stopped for a chat, I must confess,
In its tiny voice, it wished me success!

Bushes rustle with secrets untold,
As I chase butterflies brave and bold,
But alas! A bee joins the whimsical chase,
As I leap and swirl, what a wild race!

Then I spotted a sign, my heart filled with dread,
"Beware of the goose!" it carefully read,
But there was no fear — I chuckled and trod,
What could be worse than the teasing of God!

Amidst the green where giggles abound,
I skated on grass, lost but still found,
With nature's jests brightening the day,
I'm the jester of woods, come what may!

Whispers of the Foggy Shore

A seagull stole my sandwich, oh dear,
With a squawk and a flap, it disappeared.
The lighthouse keeper's pants were too tight,
He couldn't run fast, what a comical sight!

The shells all giggle as they roll in the tide,
Playing hide and seek, they just can't decide.
A crab in a top hat danced by the net,
Who knew crustaceans could be such a threat?

Waves brought in gossip from distant lands,
Of seaweed parties and wild rubber bands.
The sandcastles grin with their turrets so tall,
But they're wary of waves, that can make them fall!

So let us frolic with joy by the shore,
Where laughter and tides give us tales galore.
With fog rolling in, the fun's just begun,
In this grand coastal circus, we're all having fun!

Secrets Beneath Salty Veils

A fish with a mustache swam to the beat,
Claiming he taught the sea turtles to cheat.
The seaweed whispered secrets, oh so sly,
While dolphins told jokes that made sailors cry.

A clam wearing glasses was reading a book,
About mermaids that knit from the sea's finest look.
The starfish giggled, saying, "Look at us shine!"
As they gossiped like crabs, feeling simply divine.

The octopus juggled with shells and a net,
His act brought applause, though he was quite wet.
The gulls held a concert, out on the sand,
With tunes that turned crabs into the band!

So dance with the waves in this watery land,
Where secrets and laughter go hand in hand.
With every splash and wave's playfully sway,
Let the salty veils show us how to play!

Echoes in the Coastal Breeze

The wind told a tale of a quirky young seal,
Who thought he could dance but had no sense of heel.
He tripped on a jellyfish, oh what a sight,
While fish laughed so hard, they knew it was right!

A pelican strutted with style and flair,
His hat made of sea foam was beyond compare.
He claimed he was royalty of the sea floor,
Until a wave knocked him down—oh, what a chore!

The sand formed a slide for the children to ride,
With laughter erupting from every side.
Seashells applauded as they rolled in delight,
In a carnival atmosphere, sparkling bright.

So let's cherish the echoes that carry our cheer,
With sea creatures living their lives without fear.
At the shore where the breezes are bonkers and bold,
Find joy in the stories that never grow old!

Shadows that Dance on Hidden Sands

The shadows of crabs held a dance-off so fun,
With each little twirl, they shone like the sun.
A riddle was posed by the wise old seaweed,
But the answer was lost, oh, what a mislead!

A turtle in shades strolled down the warm strip,
Claiming he came straight from "Coolest of Hip."
But everyone knew he'd just taken a nap,
While dreaming of being the best in the clap!

The waves whispered secrets and tickled the shore,
Inviting all creatures to come join the score.
With stars as their lights, the night turned so grand,
As shadows of laughter danced over the sand.

So let's raise a toast to the silliness here,
With giggles and shadows that fill us with cheer.
In the place where the tides make the silliest plans,
We'll all join the dance on these hidden sands!

Lullabies of the Marine Twilight

In the bay, a fish does dance,
Wearing shades, he takes a chance.
Seaweed tickles crabs in line,
They giggle loud, oh what a sign!

A seagull sings a funny tune,
While jellyfish float like a balloon.
The starfish prance in silly shoes,
Tickling waves and sharing views.

A turtle spins in joyful play,
Chasing shadows, come what may.
Octopus juggles shells with flair,
While clams clap hands, a wild affair.

So close your eyes, let laughter roam,
In sea-swept dreams, we find our home.
With waves that laugh and breezes sweet,
Marine twilight hums a fun heartbeat.

Serenity in the Cloak of Ocean Haze

The lighthouse beams a quirky grin,
As dolphins giggle, splash, and spin.
A crab snaps jokes, quite punny you see,
While the sun bows low, sipping sweet tea.

The mist rolls in, a fluffy thrill,
A squid in disguise, what a quirky chill.
Mermaids frolic, with hair like foam,
Splashing the sailors who wander home.

An octopus tries a funny dance,
With eight left feet, he's got no chance.
Pufferfish puff in a comical way,
Blowing bubbles, come what may.

So snuggle tight in your warm bed,
Picture the sea with laughter ahead.
For in the haze, joy floats like a kite,
Serenity wrapped in humor's light.

The Enchanted Isle's Veil

Upon the shore, a crab finds shoes,
Racing the tide while making news.
A parrot pipes funny tales of lore,
As parrots often do, who could ask for more?

The island mist hides a coconut spy,
Napping until the tide comes by.
Funny fish swim with a silly wink,
Stirring the seaweed, they giggle and wink.

At twilight time, the stars arrive,
A glowworm party, oh what a hive!
Seahorses dance in a wobbly jig,
Bouncing along, so bright and big.

So let your worries drift away,
In enchanted laughter, let's sway.
This isle in mist, where fun prevails,
Tells tales of joy beneath its veils.

Glistening Pearls of Morning Dew

The dawn breaks with a silly yawn,
Pearls of dew grace the waving lawn.
A flamingo's strut steals the show,
While ducks quack jokes, just so you know.

The sun peek-a-boos through the trees,
Like an old trickster on a breeze.
Shells giggle softly, washed in glee,
As starfish plan a wild jubilee.

The waves tickle toes with a splash,
As pelicans glide, quick in a dash.
Morning laughter sparks in the air,
With all the creatures joining the fair.

So cherish each moment, light as air,
In droplets of fun, not a worry to bear.
For glistening pearls with laughter do brew,
A joyful symphony, fresh and new.

Between Fog and Shore

In the fog, a crab wears a hat,
Strutting about, looking quite fat.
Seagulls squawk with gossiping glee,
While jellyfish dance in the sea's jubilee.

A turtle snoozes, dreams of a race,
While lighthouses play hide and chase.
Mermaids giggle, knitting with kelp,
As waves crash and chuckle, 'What's the help?'

The sun peeks through, a cheeky grin,
Waving hello, let the shenanigans begin.
Frogs in capes leap from rock to rock,
While fish form a band with their own tick-tock.

The tide rolls in with a playful shove,
As seaweed wreaths everyone it loves.
Adventures bloom on this silly stage,
Where laughter rides every tidal wave.

Haze upon the Forgotten Isle

In the haze, a pirate with socks,
Tries to navigate with a chicken in box.
His crew of goats just munch and chew,
While the compass spins out of the blue.

Trees wiggle, tickled by the breeze,
Whispering secrets with utmost ease.
"Arrr, matey!" the goats bleat in jest,
As treasure maps lead them on a quest.

A coconut falls, causing a fuss,
It bounces 'round like a bus on a bus.
The pirate just laughs, spills mead on his chin,
While crabs hold a court, they've got him pinned!

Finally, the fog lifts, and what do they see?
A pie on the beach with "Eat Me" decree!
They dive in headfirst, as laughter takes flight,
On this hazy isle, everything's bright.

Enigmas Wrapped in Gossamer

Wrapped in whispers of thin, gauzy threads,
The ghost of a fish tells tales in beds.
With a gurgling laugh, it spins a yarn,
About soggy socks and a scaly barn.

A butterfly briefly drifts through the smoke,
Tickling a starfish who then starts to poke.
"I'm the captain!" claims a floating marshmallow,
As crabs do the can-can upon a swell shallow.

A riddle unfurls in the nets of the tide,
"Why did the clam not want to hide?"
"Because it saw a shrimp doing the limbo,
And joined in too, with a hearty 'Bingo!'"

The gossamer glimmers with humor unseen,
As creatures of water partake in the scene.
In this realm of whimsy, where laughter's the cost,
Mysteries unravel with giggles embossed.

Shades of the Shimmering Horizon

On the horizon, a fish paints a hue,
Of polka dots, pink, and a splash of blue.
With a cheeky grin, it debates the sun,
"Catch me if you can, let's have some fun!"

Turtles in sunglasses flip-flop to shore,
Practicing poses, "Look at me, score!"
A wave rolls in, an unexpected guest,
And sweeps them off with laughter's request.

Octopuses juggle, all eight arms in play,
While a conch shells tells gossip on parade.
"Did you hear?" it whispers, "About the crab who sings?
It thinks it's a star, with bling and all things!"

As twilight settles with quirky delight,
Creatures caper and twirl in the light.
Beneath the hues of twilight's embrace,
Fun ripples wide in this magical space.

The Hidden Heart of the Ocean

A crab wore glasses, reading a map,
It thought it found treasure, but took a nap.
A seagull laughed, feeling quite spry,
While fish did the tango, just passing by.

The waves told secrets, a riddle or two,
While dolphins played poker, calling you 'blue.'
Octopuses juggled, much to our surprise,
And mermaids sang songs with potato chip fries.

Sandcastles melted, they giggled and sighed,
As the tide rolled in, their kingdom denied.
With shells for a crown, they put on a show,
As beachgoers shrieked from the tickling flow.

A Symphony of Fog and Dream

In a foggy concert, the owls hoot loud,
While raccoons in tuxedos gather a crowd.
A symphony plays on the misty guitar,
As ants tap-dance under moonlight's bright star.

The trees sway gently, keeping the beat,
While frogs croak notes from their marshy seat.
An orchestra forms, with bugs in the back,
Conducted by fireflies buzzing in black.

As the sun starts to rise, the music won't cease,
The critters are playing for joy, not for peace.
With laughter and rhythm, they dance and they swirl,
Turning the fog into sparkles that twirl.

Embracing the Echoes of Silence

A clam told a joke, it got quite a laugh,
The shrimp was too busy calculating math.
An old turtle chimed in, wise with a spin,
"You know, folks, it's not just the shell that you win!"

The seaweed was dancing, twirling with flair,
While jellyfish floated without a care.
For those in the silence, they laughed and they played,
Echoes of giggles were beautifully laid.

With whispers of waves and secrets so bright,
The octopus winked in the soft moonlight.
The silence embraced them, like a warm hug,
As they reveled in joy like a well-loved bug.

Luminous Shadows Amid the Fog

In shadows all lit by the glow of the night,
A lobster wore shades and danced with delight.
A walrus, quite dapper, played hide-and-seek,
While the dolphins all snickered, 'He'll never peek!'

Fog drifted softly, with hints of a laugh,
While a crab played chess with a polka dot giraffe.
The shadows entwined in a whimsical plot,
Creating a banter as lively as hot.

The flickering lights, like stars in disguise,
Made jokes of the sea and the depth of the skies.
As the night wore on, every creature agreed,
Silhouetted in humor, they danced to their creed.

Reflections on the Shrouded Waters

In watery glass we see a face,
It's a mermaid who forgot her place.
She's lost her comb and misplaced her song,
Now she's here singing all night long.

Fish are gossiping, we hear their tales,
Of turtles in hats and dolphins with scales.
Seagulls are laughing, they can't take flight,
While the octopus dances, it's quite the sight.

Bubbles trapped in a floating hat,
A crab steals lunch, now how about that?
The wind whispers jokes to the reeds nearby,
While the seashells giggle, "Oh my, oh my!"

So come explore these shimmering skies,
Where silliness splashes, goodness multiplies.
For in the reflections of watery cheer,
Lies humor that twinkles, bright and clear.

The Soft Embrace of Dawn

The sun yawns wide, stretching its beams,
While the ocean giggles, washing dreams.
Pelicans waddle with breakfast in mind,
Bargaining clams, so generous and kind.

The sandcastles built with grand little moats,
Collapse with a giggle, like silly old goats.
Seagulls are squawking, 'What's for brunch today?'
While the ocean's laughing, 'I made a souffle!'

Starfish are lazy, stuck to the floor,
As waves tickle toes with a splash and a roar.
Shells play tag, rolling into each other,
Complaining of crabs who are being a bother.

Dawn brings a chuckle with hues that amuse,
Painting the skies in bright yellows and blues.
Join the fandango, embrace the day's light,
With laughter that dances from morning till night.

Shadows Dance in the Iris Twilight

In twilight's embrace where shadows creep,
Critters are sneaking, trying not to peep.
Owls have the fashion, cloaked in their air,
While the raccoons prance without a care.

Fireflies flicker like stars that fell,
They light up the night with a giggly spell.
Frog in a tux hits the dance floor bold,
While the pond plays music that's never old.

Bats in the belfry chuckle and glide,
Mixing up magic with a broomstick ride.
Whispers of mischief, a soft-spoken breeze,
Merging with laughter that never quite leaves.

As night wraps us up in its cozy quilt,
The shadows play tricks, their mischief is built.
With each little giggle, a teardrop will spark,
In twilight's embrace, let's laugh in the dark.

Wandering Souls of the Tidal Realm

From the deepest tides, they come and they go,
With flippers and fins, putting on quite the show.
A narwhal's a unicorn, don't you believe?
In this magical world, you've got to perceive.

Clams hold their meetings with a perky old grin,
While sea cucumbers laugh at the din.
Anemones wave their tentacles high,
As jellyfish float by, giving nods as they fly.

Starfish are common, but oh so unique,
They gather for stories, all of them peak.
Turtles exchange jokes that take quite some time,
In the sea's bustling market, where laughter's a rhyme.

So wander these waters, let the fun begin,
With tales from the depths, your lessons within.
For wandering souls in this tidal domain,
Find laughter as jewels that never grow vain.

Island Reveries in Silver Haze

A crab in a tux, what a sight to see,
Dancing on sand, as happy as can be.
He twirls with a shell, on a stage of the tide,
Laughing at seagulls, who just want to hide.

A parrot pops popcorn, oh what a delight,
He throws it to fish, who munch in the night.
The palm trees are swaying with grace and with flair,
As the moon spins a tale in the cool evening air.

A flip-flop is lost, it floats like a boat,
While a starfish steals it, oh what a hoat!
The jellyfish giggle, wearing jelly hats,
Practicing dances with loose-fitting bats.

In dreams made of sand, we frolic and play,
Wishing for breakfast, a coconut buffet.
With laughter that echoes, the memories blend,
On this whimsical isle, where antics won't end.

Lacing Dreams of Twilight Shores

The sun takes a tumble, falling in a rush,
While dolphins wear sunglasses and start off with a hush.
Flip-flops are flopping, a conch shell's intrigue,
As crabs form a band, a colorful league.

In the twilight's embrace, the laughter begins,
As turtles do ballet, with tickles and spins.
Bubbles rise up, like cheers from the sea,
While fish sport the latest in oceanic spree.

A beach ball escapes, bouncing past a palm,
It plays tag with the waves, oh what a charm!
The moon's just a nose, peeking through the mist,
As gulls share a joke, none dare to resist.

Mirth is the treasure, on shores gleaming bright,
With sandcastles dancing till the stars beam their light.
In laughter and whispers, this joy we adore,
As dreams lace the twilight, on the golden shore.

Lost in Whispers of the Ocean

A crab invented fashion, with shells of great flair,
He hosted a party, with laughter to spare.
The fish wore sequins, as bright as the sun,
While starfish took selfies, just having some fun.

Waves play hide-and-seek, with seaweed galore,
As mermaids sip smoothies, making quite a score.
A clam starts to sing, tunes from the deep,
While octopi juggle, oh what antics they keep!

In the shimmer of water, all worries take flight,
The sand tickles toes in the soft, dim moonlight.
With laughter and joy echoing so clear,
The whispers of ocean bring magic right near.

With treasures so silly, life's antics abound,
As gulls share their secrets, upon the soft ground.
In this merry realm, no frowns shall be found,
Just joy in each wave, as laughter resounds.

Serenade of the Hidden Coast

The tide creaks a joke, with a wink from the sea,
Fish hold their bellies, and giggle with glee.
A starfish, quite witty, wears spectacles proud,
Dropping punchlines that echo, loud in the crowd.

In a shell-like café, sea turtles do dine,
On seaweed delights, washed down with some brine.
Each wave brings a chuckle, as humor awakes,
In this giggling realm, where the sea always shakes.

The crabs march in rhythm, a quirky parade,
With flippers and fins, they dance unafraid.
Mermaids in laughter, twirl with carefree spins,
While dolphins compose jigs with flute-like fins.

In the sea's silly song, we all blend with cheer,
Hidden treasures of joy, that draw us all near.
So let's raise a shell with laughter that's tossed,
Celebrating the finest delight we won't lost.

Luminescence of Lost Islands

A coconut fell with a thud,
Right on a crab in the mud.
It blinked and it waved,
As if it was saved.

The palm trees danced to a tune,
While a parrot squawked at the moon.
"We're having a party!" he cried,
As the ocean waves teased the tide.

In the distance, a ship sailed by,
Chasing dreams under the sky.
With fish that wore hats and ties,
And seagulls with clever replies.

At dusk, everyone shared a laugh,
The dolphins invented their own math.
Counting stars on the shell,
Life's a joke, after all, can't you tell?

Elysium Hidden in Silver Haze

A turtle wore spectacles bright,
To read tales of fish in the night.
With a wink and a nod,
He played the old cod.

The waves whispered secrets so dear,
While a dolphin drank up all the beer.
"I'm the king!" he proclaimed,
As the seaweed laughed, unashamed.

A crab tapped his feet to the sound,
Of a clam who was quite renowned.
"Let's dance on the coral floor,
And perhaps we'll find treasure galore!"

So they twirled and they spun till they dropped,
While the jellyfish laughed, never stopped.
In this paradise, joy was the maze,
Crafting memories in silver haze.

Fables Carried by the Misty Breeze

A wise old owl made a toast,
To a clam who was known as the host.
"You're the shellfish with flair,
Who brings laughter to air!"

The breeze giggled, tickling the leaves,
As gossip spread 'bout the cats on the eaves.
"Mittens caught a big fish,
But it's still on his dish!"

A raccoon danced in moonlight's embrace,
While a seal tried to keep up the pace.
With a splash and a slide,
Everyone laughed, eyes open wide.

Thus tales were spun 'neath the stars,
Of friends and excitement shared from afar.
In this kingdom of joy, no one grieves,
As fables float high, carried by leaves.

The Tides of Hope on Soft Shores

Once, a crab had a splendid dream,
Of catching a wave like a stream.
But instead, he just rolled,
In the sand, so bold.

There came a fish with a crown,
Who thought he was the talk of the town.
"I'm royalty here!" he'd boast,
While flounders just laughed, toasting toast.

The seagulls played tag with the breeze,
As the sun haphazardly teased.
"Life's a wave!" they all chirped,
As the horizon twinkled and burped.

At dusk, they all gathered in cheer,
With tales that had everyone near.
For in this soft shore sunset glow,
Hope comes and goes, a funny show.

www.ingramcontent.com/pod-product-compliance
Lightning Source LLC
Chambersburg PA
CBHW072117070526
44585CB00016B/1477